SUMMER OF YOUTH

A COLLECTION OF POEMS

SHIVANI VERMA

I dedicate this book to my youth.

Thank you for all these adventures.

Contents

Foreword

I am not expert but fan of poetry. This collection of poems are wonderful. These poems are so mesmerising. Though writer is beginner but she tried so well to write sweetly and imaginatively all her thoughts. I'm embarrassed to admit but damn, this is so good. Trust me, this is not that boring. I can assure you.

You can take out some time from your busy schedule to read this. This can make you feel tickle and feel the warmth at the same time. This is worth reading.

Riya

(loyal reader)

Acknowledgements

First of all, I would like to thank Almighty for bringing me this close to my dream. Thank you universe for imparting hope and courage in me to grab this opportunity.

I am very thankful to my family who helped me to write this book and encouraged me in so many ways. Without their continual support this wouldn't have happened. Because they all are my loyal readers.

I have to mention names of my sisters Naina, Riya and Priyanka because they all helped me in editing though it was not that perfect. Thank you for all your efforts. And my brothers Anmol and Aditya thank you for helping me with the designs. Thank you God for blessing me with so many gifts.

Oh, how can I forget to thank the most important companions of my journey my pets Casper, Pepper, Julie and Mao. I am so much thankful for their disturbance and love. They all are such an important crew of my life.

At last , I wish to express my thank to each and everyone who was ever the part of my life. Thank you all for creating moments of my life which helped me to discover myself.

1. FIRST LOVE

Wanna hold you like this cup of wine,
sipping and melting the taste of your love in my mind.
lingering to your silence,
Breaking all your inner rhymes.
Embracing your heart,
just by looking into your eyes.
Appreciating the taste of your fragrance,
like how I appreciate the flavour of this wine.
Reminiscing the tale of our lives,
And pairing with you
like this cake who accompanies this cup of wine.
drinking for the thousand nights
And not getting drunk.
Because it's not intoxicating as your eyes.

2. LOOK INTO MY EYES

Look into my eyes,
You'll find depth deeper than the ocean,
And light brighter than the meteorites,
warmth better than the sun.
love and compassion
Solving many mysterious vibes.
It's your charm which give them uniqueness.
forget your allergy to show love ,
Look for better horizon
to watch more beautiful sunrise.
I can see into you through your eyes.
they are enough to tell ,
because they are the mirror of your soul .
Stop hiding, you cannot bear the price
look into my eyes,
You'll find depth deeper than the ocean
And light brighter than meteorites.

3. SIT WITH GRIEF

I sit with grief and hear it say,
Why is it so hard to find the way?
same question, same confusion and same pain.
I wander all night looking for the calling way,
I was working when you slept in daze.
Worrying about the world's business,
I couldn't sleep for many nights.
I felt like resigning,
from this tiring job of searching light.
I was shocked, having no courage to face
I rejected the idea to believe what they say.
Ray of pain and guilt peeped in,
I was cursing myself for being so lame
I desired for time travel,
But my efforts went in vain.
I was pleading and bargaining,
shedding tears in many rain.
Nothing worked I got anger in pale.
I was clinging and scolding who is up there ,
No answer came.
Sitting all alone in corner of heart,
I was just thinking about my pain.

reminiscing all the memories again and again.
I got fed and decided to change
"Don't worry." said to my heart
And dedicated myself to find some way.
Reconstructed all the ideas and beliefs
Corrected all my mischievous mistakes
I looked for the hope ,
And worked for the better game.
There is nothing I could do ,
except accepting all what has changed.

4. GROWTH

I feel like universe is growing inside me,
pampering all it's edges,
filling the oasis of it's desert,
covering all the unpainted murals,
Igniting the flames of passion,
Resisting all the barriers
And walking along the carriers.
experiencing the different galaxies.
Sometime enjoying the thrills of parallel universe
and finding some answers with time travel.
Getting little joys of life,
act as adrenaline rush
adding fuel to my life.
though they pass
but leave their beautiful essence
to ask for more.
I feel like universe is growing inside me.
I feel like universe is growing inside me.

5. DREAM

Once, I had a dream
I wanted to fly in the space,
Watching all those galaxies, stars and meteorites
wondering if I could meet some aliens
Dreaming to see the Saturn's rings
Sitting under the night sky
And watching till so late
I was so crazy,
got this dream from a story
With time, I found
this dream is not for me
Once it was part of me,
was so desperate to achieve.
I tried with all best I have.
But couldn't pass .
got indulged in many new dreams
developed new skills
And forgot my sparkling dream
left my stars and galaxies
felt bad for forgetting
that regret stayed in the corner of my heart for too long,
I got tired of it

And burnt it because I don't need it anymore
Voice inside questioned me, Why you wanted it before?
"It was just the implication of fantasy", my head replied.
Some parts of it are still with me
I give life to them
by doing what I can.
spending long hours under that midnight sky
reading those constellations
watching satellites and greeting all those flights
And that rush to see falling stars
I enjoy viewing them
even appreciate their beauty.
On appropriate time,
maybe I can make some efforts for it
but will take some time
While other half of this dream
is too much for me
I visit it often in my mind
Pay some condolences
And revise my lessons
for now,
All I can say is
I am okay with this,
I don't need that broken dream
It is just a dream.
It is just a dream

6. HEART FILLED WITH HOPE

My heart filled with hope
that is deep
touching warmth of my soul
impacting
which is deeper than the mines
even if read for
thousands of time
still felt the same like first time
I wish it to be long lasting song
not afraid of fears, tears and regrets
even with broken wings ,
who dares to fly high
Following the light
and forgetting all the egos i have
walking in river of life
not in vain
to see many unseen
And never feeling lonely
passing all the cold winds
forgetting the arrogant

memories of past,
making my appearance
more stubborn and bold.
My heart filled with hope
I want to cherish it
as whole

7. LETTER TO MY CHILDHOOD

You were the sweetest time,
lingering with fragrance of innocence
and giving positive vibes
all those doubts and fears
which I passed
made me what I am
I cherish those memories like old treasure
They fill me with inspirations and aspirations.
Those morning walks
visiting temple for exams
playing hopscotch on street
and climbing on those garden trees
Failed attempts to make Christmas cake
being daring singer only in bathroom space
All those days of silly friendship vows
and now they all are lost
No worries , no race
they were all the days of simplicity and innocent face
lessons were taught
Which I can never forgot

I am grateful for your call
it reminded me of beautiful time zone

8. LETTER TO MY PEPPER

You were tiny and soft
at first sight that I caught
Cuddling around your siblings
your eyes were tightly closed
You were living in my home
along with your mom
born in that peaceful summer
you all were so cute
those four months you were with us
But after that one day
because of sudden sickness
You got injections for days
but you couldn't be saved
You were on my lap when you left
But you were amazing soul
I can never forget
your memories
because they are strengthening me
I felt so blessed
when you use to sit to pray with me

falling asleep on my meditation mat
And that your hobby of
following me everywhere
And waiting for me to come when I go for outing for days
silently enjoying the winter sun with me
little champ all your little acts
filled my heart with gratitude
I can never forget
You are part of me,
that can never be made apart

9. MY YOUTH

These days of youth
full of dazzling life,
very naughty, tough and wild
most of time lost in books
and for other behaving like crazy wild
lots of hope and devotion
could be seen in eyes
not afraid of challenges
always fighting for right
curious to learn something new
and reading for long hours
standing up for being independent
holding that desire
to be the highness of my own life
keep going on harsh days
And keeping that hope alive
This youth is full of expeditions of discovering more
creating identity of me as the part of whole
These days of youth
will be my story
which I can read for thousand times
telling to all

who will come across
telling my numerous shades
And enthusiasm that never fades
These days of youth
will keep pushing me toward my goals.
they define me to all.

10. LAST GOODBYE

On my death bed I would like to see you
embracing my body in your arms,
shedding tear drops from my eyes.
I would be telling you thousands of tales,
with just blink of my eyes.
liberating my soul in presence of your sight
would be the best gift of divine.
Watching your torn heart,
I will be pleading ,
let's not rush to make us apart.
wishing to be deaf
to those summons from the world afar.
I will clinge to illimitable happiness of our past.
I will be holding to our memories
and repeating those murky episodes of our lives.
Expressing my gratitude ,
I will be kissing your sigh.
Little selfish part of me would expect
you to love me each second of your life.
And other will ask you to let go ,
asking to find new love and life.
At first, there would be struggle

and grief accepting the fact.
Even the thought of separation seems horrifying
But after constant denial,
When the last breath comes,
meandering emptiness will surround.
And I will bid you goodbye packed with love.
And I will bid you goodbye packed with love.